When I grow up

I want to be a builder
working to a plan.

I want to be a tourist guide,
take people to Japan.

I want to be an astronaut
with badges on my gear.

I want to be an author,
write a new book every year!

What do you want to be? What writing will you do in your job?
Draw and write about your dream job.

Contents and curriculum links

Page number		Content	Eng Language	Eng Literature	Eng Literacy	History	Maths	Science	Other
1		*When I grow up* poem		•	•				
2		Contents and curriculum links			•				
3		Getting ready to write	•		•				
4		Concepts of writing	•		•				
5		Purpose of writing	•		•				
6		Letter formation: cursive style	•		•				
7		Instructions: Anti-clockwise and clockwise formation	•		•				
8		Instructions: Downward letter formation	•		•				
9		Reference: Starting point and direction	•		•				
10	a	Types of apples	•		•	•		•	H & P E
11	b	Brushes	•		•			•	
12	Fl.	Braille	•		•	•			
13	c	Cinderella	•	•	•				
14	d	*Dinosaur* poem	•		•			•	
15	Fl.	Riddle	•		•				
16	e	Equator	•		•			•	Geog
17	f	Riddle	•		•				
18	g	Gorillas	•		•			•	
19	Fl.	Word building	•		•				
20	h	Heliograph	•		•	•		•	Tech
21	i	Traditional rhyme	•		•				
22	WYO	Crossword	•		•				
23	j	Meaning of January	•		•	•			
24	k	The sound 'k'	•		•				
25	Fl.	Car dashboard controls	•		•			•	Tech
26	l	Lines	•		•		•		
27	m	Riddles	•		•				
28	n	Meaning of neighbour	•		•				
29	Fl.	Making a book	•		•				Tech
30	o	Silly rhyme	•		•				
31	p	Making prints	•		•				Art
32	Fl	Square and triangular numbers	•		•		•		
33	q	Invented words	•		•				
34	r	Riddle	•	•	•				
35	WYO	Compound words	•		•				
36	s	Animal actions	•		•			•	
37	t	TV history	•		•	•			
38	WYO	Instructions	•		•				Art
39	u	Word trail	•		•				
40	v	Volcanoes	•		•			•	Geog
41	WYO	Write questions for these answers	•		•				
42	w	Riddles	•		•				
43	x	Words inside words	•		•				
44	WYO	Descriptive writing	•		•				
45	y	Explanation about onions	•		•			•	
46	z	Zips	•		•			•	
47	WYO	Build-a-story	•		•				
48		End of year assessment	•		•				

Fl. = Fluency page   WYO = Write Your Own page

1 Hold your pencil like this.

Hold it **lightly** so your hand doesn't get tired.

2 Sit facing your desk, or turn slightly.
Turn your paper also.

Right-handers sit like this.

3 Keep your hand **below** the writing line so that you can see what you are writing.
Rest your other arm on the desk.

Try not to write across your body. Keep the paper on the side of your body that you write with.

Left-handers sit like this.

Concepts of writing

Writing is made up of letters and words.

Letters c e g k m s t w

Words brush pencil scissors

Sentences I like painting.

Did you paint your house?

Letters make different sounds in different words.
English has 26 letters. They can be written in CAPITALS or lower case.

Spaces between the words make it easier to read the writing.

A sentence is a group of words that makes a whole thought or idea.
Sentences start with a capital letter and usually end with a full stop or a question mark.

Purpose of writing

Writing is very useful.

You can …

describe things

keep a diary

explain ideas

write instructions

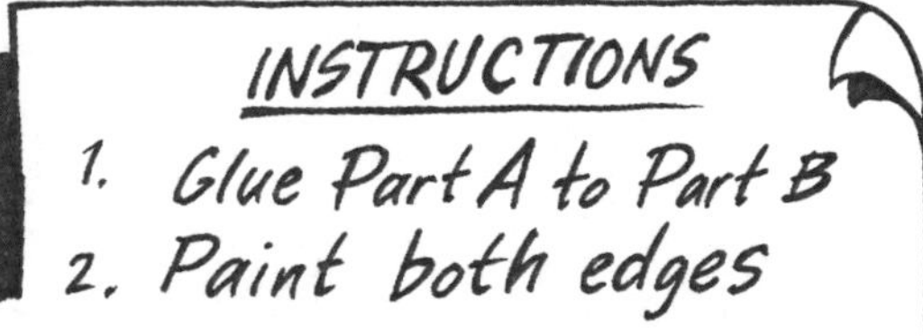

tell stories

leave messages

make lists

label things

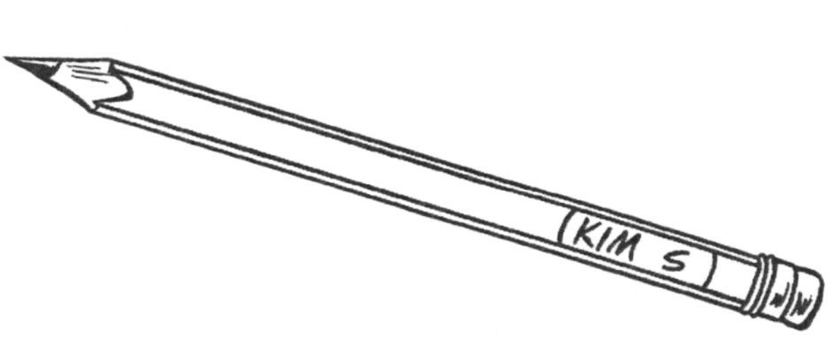

and have fun!

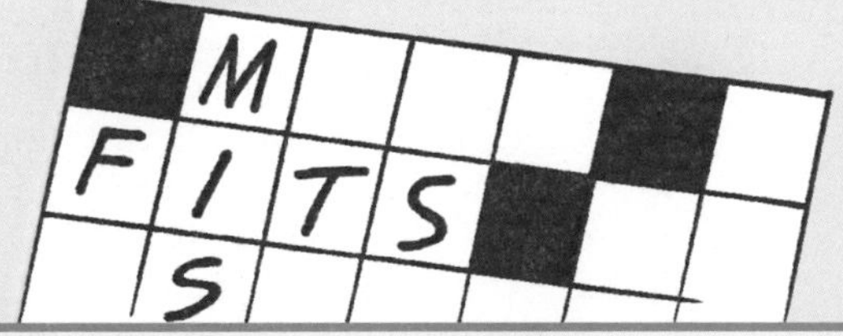

1 Most letters start at the **top** and have strong **down strokes.**

h j l o u

2 Most letters have **crisp** turns. This makes a **wedge** shape inside many letters.

e t v d n

3 Many letters have **exits** and some have **entries**. This makes it easier to do joined writing later on.

a k m r t

4 The writing has a slight **slope** to help with fluency. You may write straight up and down if you prefer.

pear tree

5 All letters have a **body**. Some also have a **head** or a **tail**. The letter **f** has all three.

c e n o s w f

b d l t g p y

Anti-clockwise letters a c g q d e o f s

a c g q

Start at the top (1 o'clock).
Move anti-clockwise.
Finish letters **a** and **q** with an exit.

d e

Start in the middle.
Move anti-clockwise.
Finish with an exit.

o f s

Start at the top.
Move anti-clockwise.
Letter **o** has an exit.
Letter **f** has a tail and two strokes.

Move anti-clockwise.
1 o'clock start
12
9
3
6
wedge exit
crisp turns

9 o'clock start
12
9
3
6
crisp turn

Clockwise letters m n r x z h k p

m n r

Start with a small entry.
Move down, then clockwise.
Finish with an exit.

x z

Start with a small entry.
Move clockwise.
Letter **x** has two strokes.
Letter **z** has a flattened tail.

h k p

Start at the top.
Move down, then clockwise.
Finish with an exit.

wedge
small rounded entry
crisp turn
exit

small rounded entry
crisp turns
flattened tail

Downward letters: the *i* family i l t j

i l t

Start at the top.
Move ↓ downwards.
Finish with an exit.
Letter **t** has two strokes.

First stroke finishes with exit.
Add dot after downward stroke.
crisp turn
exit

j

Start at the top.
Move ↓ downwards.
Finish with a flattened tail.

First stroke finishes with exit.
Lift pen. Add second stroke.
crisp turn
exit

Downward letters: the *u* family u v w b y

u v w b

Start at the top.
Move ↓ downwards.
Use crisp turns.
Finish with an exit.

wedge
exit
crisp turns

y

Start at the top.
Move ↓ downwards.
Finish with a flattened tail.

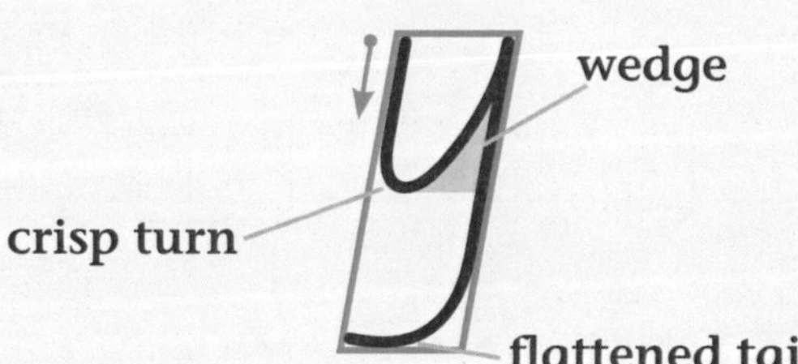

Reference: Starting point and direction

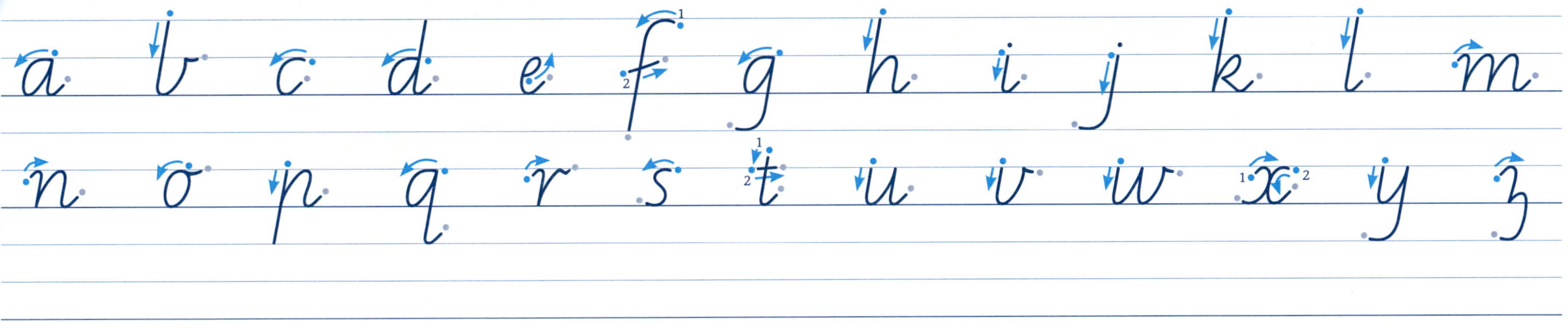

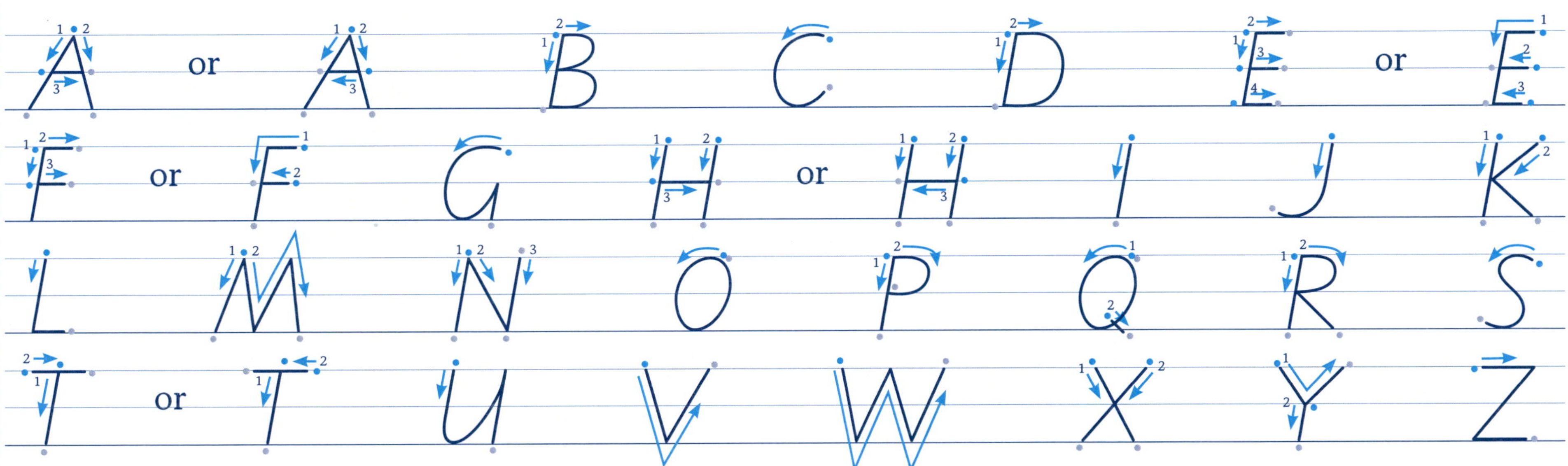

• Starting point ↓ direction • finishing point
UPPER CASE: alternative formations are for left-handers.

a a a A A

There are many types of apples.

Jonathan apples are red.

Golden delicious apples are yellow.

Granny Smith apples are green.

EXTRA: Granny Smith was a real person. What can you find out about her?

ll ll ll b b b B B

Brushes and brooms

 made of bristles, plastic, straw

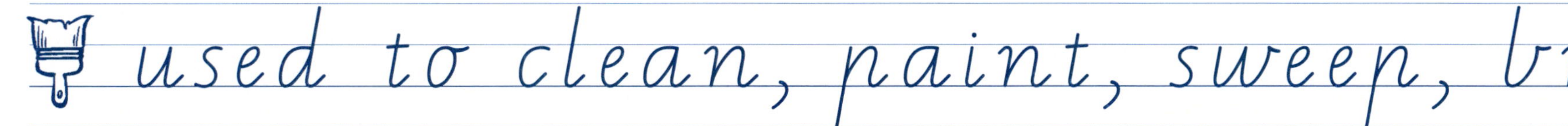

used to clean, paint, sweep, brush

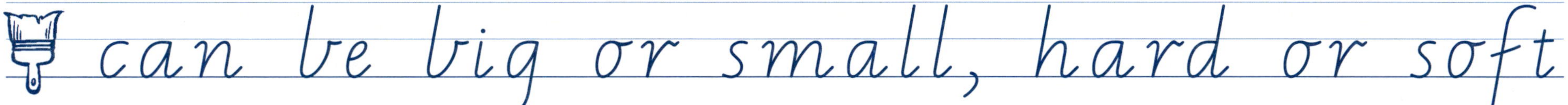

can be big or small, hard or soft

EXTRA: Make a list of different brushes and brooms and their uses.

The Braille alphabet

- for the blind and vision-impaired
- combinations of a six-dot grid

make raised letters and numbers

EXTRA: Find out about Louis Braille.

Self-assess

c c c C C

'Cinderella' is an old fairy tale about a beautiful girl and her two cruel stepsisters. Cinderella cries when she cannot go to the ball.

EXTRA: Find two different versions of the Cinderella story to read and compare.

b b b d d d D D

Dinosaur D

In the swamp I

Noisy N

Old O

Small brained S

Alive! A

Ugly? U

Really big R

EXTRA: Write a poem like this one about another animal, alive or extinct.

Fluency: Riddle

Take away my first letter,

take away my second letter,

take away all my letters,

and I'm still the same.

Who am I?

The postie!

EXTRA: Explain the double meaning in this riddle.

e e e E E

The equator is 40 076 km long.

It divides the Earth into two

halves called hemispheres.

We live in the southern hemisphere.

EXTRA: Is the equator real or imaginary? Have you ever crossed it?

ff ff f f f F F

Five fat frogs are sitting on a log,

Four decide to jump off.

How many are left?

Five.

Why? None have moved yet.

EXTRA: Try this riddle out on family and friends.

Self-assess

Gorillas are large African apes.

They are mostly vegetarian.

They live in family groups.

Males can weigh up to 300 kg.

EXTRA: Find out more about apes and other **primates**.

na nap Nat arena

ho hot house those

ie pie tries silliest

ly fly lovely sadly

th the this another

EXTRA: Can you build words with two or more of the letter clusters in the same word?

l l l l l l l l l h h h H H

A heliograph is a message,

sent a long way by

using reflected sunlight

on a movable mirror.

EXTRA: When and where might people use a heliograph?

||| ||| ||| i i i l l

It's raining, it's pouring,

the old man is snoring,

went to bed and bumped his head

and couldn't get up in the morning.

EXTRA: Write a new rhyme using other types of weather. It's hailing, it's snowing …

1 B
2 B
3 H
4
5 G R
6
7
8
9
10
11
12

Across

1 large
5 mother's mother
7 small insect that lives in colonies
8 You need one to get into the movies.
9 She doesn't like ____ carrots, she only eats them raw.
10 not wearing any clothes
12 an important place for learning

Down

1 crooked, not straight
2 The bird sat on a small ____ , out of reach of the cat.
3 when there is no school
4 This book is called ____ Well.
6 a banana, ____ apple
8 half of twenty
11 openings in house walls: windows and ____ ways

EXTRA: Write a new set of clues for this crossword.

j j j J J

January is the first month.

It is named after a Roman god.

Janus had two faces, so he could

look backwards and forwards.

EXTRA: Find out the meanings of the other months of the year.

EXTRA: Make a list of words using these spellings for the sound 'k'.

1 speedometer – rate of travel

2 odometer – distance travelled

3 tachometer – engine revs

4 thermometer – temperature

Self-assess

EXTRA: What does the *meter* part of these words mean?

Downward formation: Lines

||| ||| ||| l l l L L

Some lines are parallel*

Some are full of clothes.

Some lines make columns

And others make rows.

* Parallel lines are lines that go in exactly the same direction. e.g. train lines and writing lines.

m m m M M

1 Spell hungry horse in 4 letters.

2 What does M-O-Q spell?

3 How does music make you sick?

1 MTGG 2 cat: MOQ 3 Take away its m.

n n n N N

Origin of the word neighbour

comes from Old English

neigh from nigh – close by

bour from gebur – dweller

EXTRA: Make up a story about a neighing neighbour.

Self-assess

How to make a 32-page book

Take one sheet of paper.*

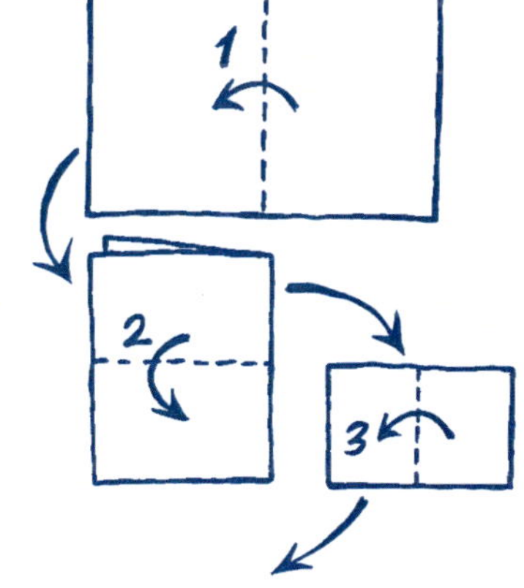

Fold it in half 4 times.

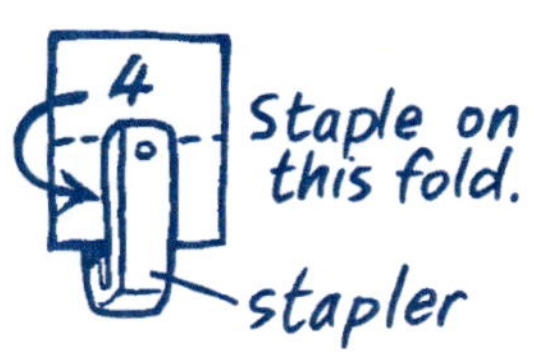

Staple the spine.

Trim the other 3 sides.

*The bigger the better: 32-page picture books are often printed on one **very** big sheet of paper.

oo oo o o o O O

Stop at the stop sign,

Go on the green.

Once around the roundabout,

Hop on the trampoline.

EXTRA: Act out this rhyme as you say it. How fast can you go?

p p p   p p p   P P

Printing – potato or sponge

string and pegs

old puzzle pieces

toothbrush splatter

EXTRA: Illustrate a story or poem using one of these techniques.

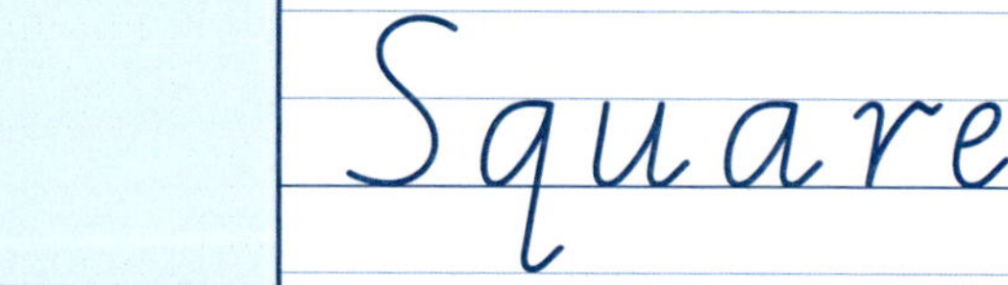

Square numbers

1 4 $(2 \times 2 = 4)$ 9 $(3 \times 3 = 9)$

16 25

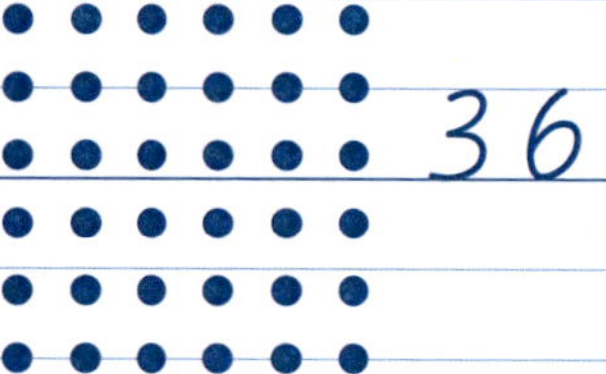

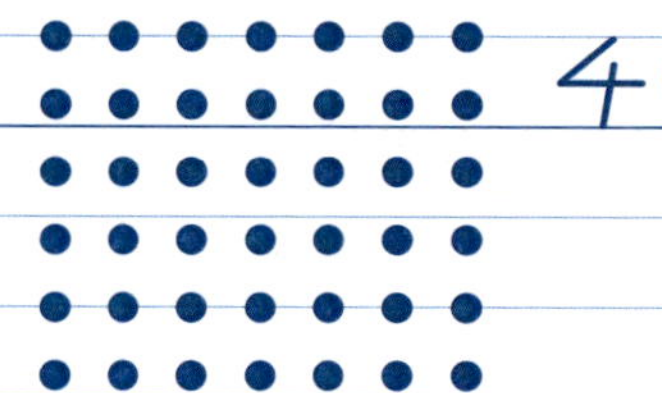

Triangular numbers

1 3 $(1 + 2 = 3)$ 6 $(1 + 2 + 3 = 6)$

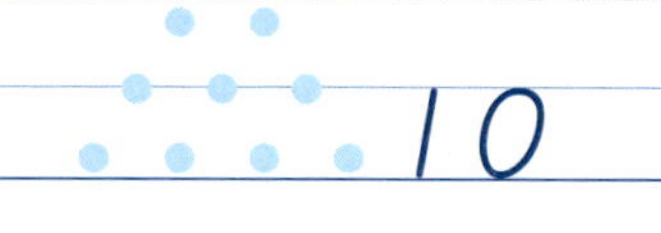

15

28

EXTRA: What comes next? Continue one of these patterns, with counters, or numbers, or both.

o o l l q q q Q Q

Not many words start with Q,

So I'm going to make up a few:

Quimp, quottle, quing, quam,

Quirry, quet, quizzle, squam!

EXTRA: These made-up words sound real enough. Make up meanings for the three you like best.

n n n r r r R R

Round and round the rugged rock

The ragged rascal ran.

How many Rs are there in that?

Now tell me if you can!

EXTRA: What country do you live in? Can you spell it?

Write your own: Compound words

Use **under** with some of the words in the box to create compound words. Then write the meaning of each one, use it in a phrase, or give an example.

under

cover	cut	done	felt	go
ground	hand	line	pants	
pass	stand	take	wear	world

Compound word	Meaning
underground	rabbits have burrows

EXTRA: Create more compound words with words in the box, using **over** or **above**.

Seagulls swoop, squabble,

Bandicoots scamper, hide.

Snakes slither, slink,

Penguins shuffle, slide.

EXTRA: Look at each verb (doing word). What other animals (including people) move this way?

Self-assess

lll lll lll t t t T T

Television in Australia

1956 — first television broadcast

1975 — first colour TV broadcast

2001 — introduction of digital TV

EXTRA: Ask family and friends about the first time they watched TV.

How to make a birthday card. Write instructions to go with each diagram.

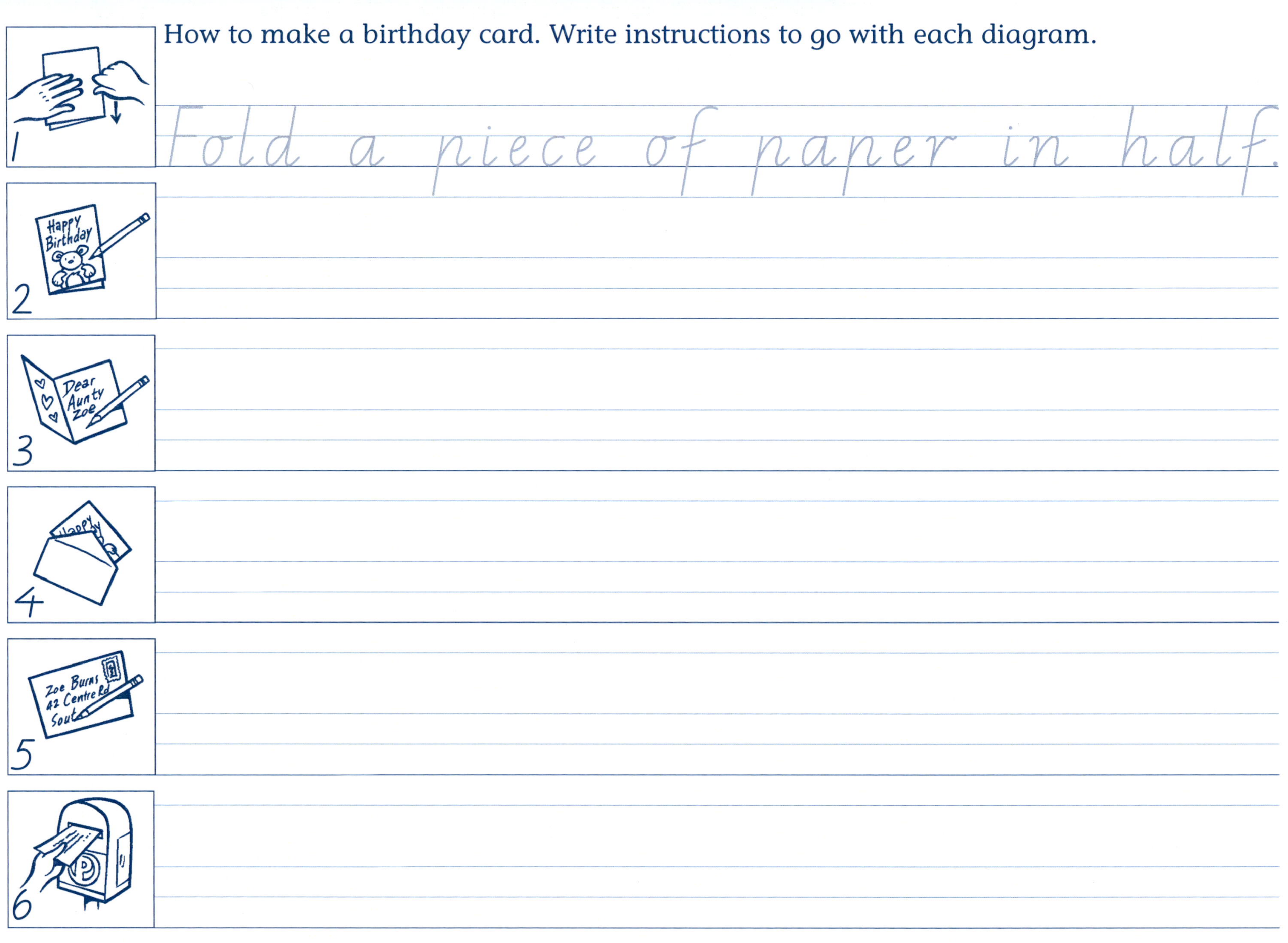

v v v u u u U U

under run number round

blur rust tugs sound

bugle emu unity yum

undid dust touch hum

EXTRA: Follow the arrows around the word trail. What are the rules? (There are at least two.)

v v v v v v V V

A volcano is an opening

in the Earth's crust.

Active volcanoes throw out gases,

lava (molten rock) or hot ash.

EXTRA: Are there active volcanoes in Australia? Are there extinct volcanoes?

Write your own: Write questions for these answers

Jan	Who lives next door?
blue	
sixty	
everyone	
home	
2 pieces	
85 cents	
to bed	
square	
the top	

EXTRA: How many different questions can you think of for the same answer?

Self-assess

w w w W W

1 What cheese is made backwards?

2 What nut grows on the wall?

3 What wobbles while it's flying?

1 Edam 2 a walnut 3 a jellycopter

xx xx xx x x x X X

Extraordinary — or extra din

Xylophone — phone one on lop

Maximum — Max Mum Ma I

Examine — exam am mine in

EXTRA: Jumble the letters to make lots more words. E.g. XYLOPHONE: hope, Leon, Noel, hole

Describe your house.
It could be a real house,
or completely made up.

MY HOUSE

Write about:
- people
- furniture
- gadgets
- colours

y y y Y Y

Why do onions make you cry?

Strong gases are released

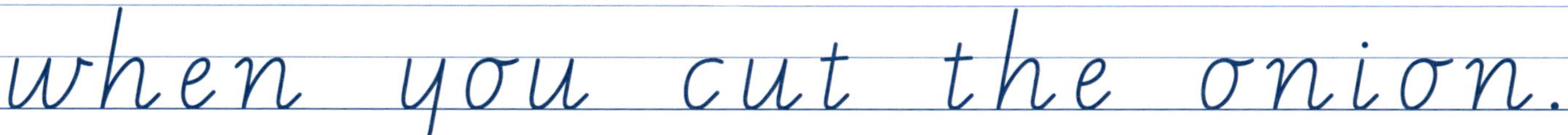

when you cut the onion.

Your tears protect your eyes.

EXTRA: Find out how to stop the tears. Ask family and friends, and research on the Internet.

z z z   z z z   Z Z

Zips have teeth.

The slider connects them.

Zips are easier to use than

buttons, studs or buckles.

EXTRA: How many things with zips do you use every day?

Write you own: Build-a-story

Write a story that has three or more of these things in it.
Look back to page 24 for the spelling of the words.

End of year assessment

1 Copy this sentence.

This is page 48 of this book.

2 Write the alphabet in lower case letters.

3 Write your name in capital letters.

4 Write a sentence about one of the things you did last weekend.